Love Letters To Teenage Motherhood

AF665105

Emma Kos

BookLeaf Publishing
India | USA | UK

Presentation by *BookLeaf Publishing*

Web: www.bookleafpub.com

E-mail: info@bookleafpub.com

ISBN: 9789357444316

First edition 2022

DEDICATION

For Catherine, whose endless support, honest opinions, constant encouragement and cover art prowess made it all happen.

ACKNOWLEDGEMENT

This book wouldn't have been possible without so many people. I am eternally grateful to everyone who has taken the time to read my stories over the years, but particularly to Kate, Em and Catherine, who have been so incredibly supportive throughout this project. To anyone who has ever encouraged me, this is for you.

PREFACE

Please note that a number of these poems contain mild references to disordered eating and self-harm which some readers may find upsetting.

Red Lines

She was just a possibility.
She was a pair of red lines on a white plastic
stick you cupped tightly between your palms;
You shivered alone in the upper school toilets,
the moment she made herself known to you.
She was a looming catastrophe.
She was a bomb due to explode right in the
middle of your Highers.
Your Highers you'd already resigned yourself to
resitting come autumn, no hope for May.
She was an abomination.
She was the scar left behind as your innocence
and your spirit were ripped from you
Pressed up against the bins in the Scotia Bar car
park, too frozen in fear to scream-
Though you didn't know it, then- her origin
story.

She was the reckless option.
She was a one-way ticket to messing up your life
for good, this time.
(Emphasis on the 'for good' part, because you
can't deny you'd messed it up all by yourself.)
She was a guaranteed route to wasted potential
and misery.

To keep her meant statistically, a downhill spiral
to dropping out of high school,
A council flat in Pollokshields, a baby of her
own by the time she was fifteen, a vicious cycle.
She was devastation.
She was the spawn of the man who turned your
world grey alive and growing inside you,
Seventeen years old and barely living, just
existing.
The pharmacist warned you the pill she placed
in your palm carried a failure rate of five
percent.

And yet she was hope.
She was a reason to sort yourself out, at last; you
were waiting outside the school library by seven
The next morning, textbooks in hand, six months
of school lost but sudden motivation in your
veins.
She was sunshine.
She was the kick up the backside you needed to
get clean, get stable, get serious about your
future-
Because when she stirred inside you, she was the
sweetest wee thing you'd ever known.
She was a future.
She was a lifetime of purpose, a warm weight
against your chest, a soft voice whispering in
your ear a name age-old, intimate, timeless.

She was a pair of red lines, but still, she was everything.
She was yours.

Responsible

You keep her a closely guarded secret for as long as you possibly can.
You're pretty sure twelve weeks is the usual point at which to make an announcement,
But you leave it far, far later than that.
It's not because you're ashamed of her.

(Is it that you're not ashamed of her, though- is that the right way to put it?
Can it even be her that you're not ashamed of when you're still carrying her inside you,
Or is it supposed to be you, your pregnancy, the situation in which you've found yourself?
Does it even matter?)

You could never, ever be ashamed of her.
She's not even born yet, admittedly, but already, you know that for certain.
You fall a little more in love with her than you ever thought possible with every kick,
Every hiccup, every unidentifiable flutter.

You just want to savour this time.
Everyone says that pregnancy is supposed to be special,

But you know full well the world will do its best
to make you feel as though it's anything but, for
you,
Just because you're still in high school.

That, and your life is a mess.
You know you're going to have to fight to get
your mum on board,
And you're completely terrified that your school
will do their worst, contact Social Services…
You can't even bear to think about what might
happen if Social Services get involved.

Keeping your pregnancy hidden until you've
sorted yourself out just seems the safest option,
And so that's exactly what you do.
It's easy enough.
Mercifully, Mother Nature seems to be on your
side.

You don't know if it's because you're barely
seventeen, a child carrying a child,
Or it's the drugs and the drink and the tobacco
smoke: all the poison
You pumped her tiny system with, before you
knew.
Or maybe she was just always going to be small.

She.

No sonographer has confirmed it,
But somehow, you know she's a girl.
You just know.

Whatever the explanation, though, you're hardly showing.
Well, you are- but it's all relative.
You're showing enough to arouse suspicion but not to the extent that it can't be concealed,
And so when you go back to school, you raid the lost property bin for a jumper three sizes too big.

Once you're hiding your changing body beneath layers of oversized clothes,
Blaming the cold chill of Scottish spring and your off-the-rails diet of chips and deep-fried mars bars,
When your mum asks, making up every excuse under the sun to get out of obligatory PE lessons,
Nobody seems to notice, and that's good enough for you.

You'll tell them all eventually.
You just want a little more time to get yourself together, stay clean, sober up,
Catch up on all the schoolwork you've missed bunking off, maybe even get yourself a Saturday job:

All the things that might convince the people
who matter that you can be a good mum.

The trouble is, you're running out of time.
She's so big, now.
You think she must be breech because she's all
up in your ribcage,
And her kicks assault your bladder so frequently
that you've used up all your spring term toilet
passes.

Sometimes, though, she makes your heart stop
with fear.
You're terrified you're going to lose her.
You know damned well you did pretty much
everything pregnant women shouldn't, before
you knew,
And you're so afraid you've done her
irreversible damage that sometimes, you can't
quite breathe.

She's everything.
She's been with you every single second of the
last thirty-two weeks,
And in that time,
You've grown dependent on her.

Every time you want to surrender,
Go back to your old coping mechanisms,

Her gentle ripples beneath your skin stop you,
Because you got yourself clean for her.

You got yourself clean, but you're so afraid you left it too late.
She goes so still, sometimes.
She goes so horribly still and in those moments, you're terrified you've lost her,
Your heart in your mouth until she stirs again, because she's all you're clinging on for.

At night, you've taken to wedging your bedroom door shut,
So your mum can't walk in unannounced
Because while you look far from close to term,
The tell-tale swell of your belly is becoming harder and harder to hide.

You'll lock yourself in your room, and time always seems to stop
When you wrap your arms around your bump, feel for her movements; no one but you and her.
You try to imagine how it might feel to hold her in your arms, and your heart just melts.
You love her so much already.

You've taken to staying on after school to tackle your homework,

Catch up with all the Highers content you've missed and work your way through practice papers
And sometimes, when you're sat in the school library she'll nudge you softly,
Almost as though she's reminding you that you can't give up now.

Because you're doing this for her.
Going back to school is possibly that hardest thing you've ever done-
Harder than getting clean, getting sober… harder than leaving the man who fathered her.
But you do it for her, to give her the best life you possibly can.

You say 'her;' in your head, she already has a name.
You've had your heart set on it ever since that first faint trait of motherly intuition kicked in
To convince you she's a girl,
But when you look up its meaning, you realise it's perfect.

She's your fresh start.
You're reborn in her, for her.
You didn't care about a goddamned thing eight months ago,

And then she came along, and everything
changed.

You've no idea how you're going to make it all
work,
When she's finally here,
But you know you will,
Because you love her too much to ever let her
down.

The final week of school before your Highers
exams,
Your Gàidhlig teacher whose departure for
maternity leave you missed
Whilst you were too busy getting high down at
the disused railway station with your baby's
father
Brings her own newborn in to show the class.

The poor wee thing is passed around the
classroom as though he's public property,
And all you can think is there's no way in hell
you'll be doing that with your own child.
Your own child…
Suddenly, it's all rather surreal.

When your turn comes you're nervous, because
it feels like something of a test.
You cradle the baby gently against your heart,

Scared to hold him too closely in case his weight
pressing into you
Highlights the secret you're still not ready to
reveal.

Your Gàidhlig teacher tells you that you're a
natural when her baby snuggles into your arms,
And for several horrible moments, you panic
that she's worked it out.
But you pass the baby on, and nothing else is
said.
Your breasts ache.

A week later, you make your first newborn
purchase.
You're in the Waitrose by the local uni campus,
Picking up the shopping your mum requested for
dinner tonight
On your way back from an open day for a course
you don't even know if you'll be able to study
with a baby.

You're gawping at the prices somewhat,
About to catch the bus back across town and
stop by Scotmid instead, when it catches your
eye.
It's an outrageously overpriced ball of white
fluff, really- and you do know that.

You were never one to find everything
baby-related adorable, until you got pregnant
with your own.

But it reminds you of your childhood,
Lambing season spent with your grandparents
on Islay and before you know it,
You're waiting at the bus stop,
Cuddly toy sheep hidden beneath your pencil
case and the open day flyers in your backpack.

You struggle to stay upright the whole journey
home in the standing area,
Centre of gravity skewed but there's no way in
hell you're confessing, asking for the priority
seat.
Just a few more weeks, you tell yourself, when
the light-headedness hits and your feet throb
persistently,
And she's kicking out furiously as though she's
telling you to slow down, let yourself rest.

It's all going to be worth it in just a few more
weeks.

In Her Father's Eyes

You didn't know, until you held her.
You couldn't have known.
That's the truth of it.
The issue of her paternity was a probability pool
of more possibilities than you ever dared admit.
You were a mess, back then.
Before her.

You held her in your arms, and she was still, at
first.
She was so still.
Born too early, the harsh, brutal chill of the
outside world seemed to paralyse her, at first.
It took her longer than it should have to breathe
air into her lungs,
but when at last she did, she opened her eyes,
and you knew.
You just knew.

Perhaps you should have felt revulsion.
(You'll spend the rest of her life arguing fiercely
that you never felt anything of the sort, of
course-
It didn't occur to you that such a reaction might
have been expected until the world told you so.)

But all you felt was a love, a protective instinct, a… a yearning, unlike anything you'd ever known.

The eyes of the monster who turned your world cold and harsh and grey
Blinked back at you in your arms,
And suddenly, the horrors of that night, the pain of leaving, the fear without him you were nothing
Faded away.

She had her father's eyes.
She had eyes as green as the meadows of her father's land- as blooming, as hopeful, as… alive
Even though in those first moments as you held her
She barely clung to life at all.

She had her father's colouring, his features, his heritage of which you knew so little,
But she smelled of you.
And so you gave her the most undeniably Scottish name you could think of,
Whispered it in her ear before the NICU team took her away.

Because in her father's eyes, there was a
gentleness you hadn't known they could hold.
She needed you.
She was so tiny, so helpless.
She needed you, and you needed her, too.

In those brief moments you held her, she fought.
She breathed.
She chose a life with you.
How could you possibly say no?

Thirty-Five Weeks, Five Days

The dull clunking of her oxygen machine is anything
But the reassuring rhythm you were promised it would be.
She's so tiny that her skin is translucent, lanugo-lined,
And her fingers and toes, her lips turned blue with cold without the gentle warming of the incubator.

She's three pounds two ounces of precious skin and bones-
She's smaller than she should be, scrawnier, oh-so fragile.
Her sucking reflex is yet to kick in and so you're struggling desperately with the breast pump,
While she fights her own battle with her nasal cannula beside you.

The obstetrician who ripped her cruelly from your arms told you she's so underdeveloped

Because you drank and smoked and your way
through your pregnancy, before you knew- and
worse.
She looked at you as though you were the scum
of the earth-
As if you don't hate yourself enough already for
the damage you've done to your wee girl.

It feels... wrong, to have her next to you,
To be separated from her by a plastic box.
You carried her inside you for thirty-five weeks,
five days,
And you miss her hiccups, her kicks, her gentle
wriggling.

All you want is to hold her in your arms.
To cuddle her.
The neonatal nurse informs you firmly that she
won't like to be touched,
But when you lay your palm across her chest,
her heart rate slows on the monitor.

So you chat away to her mindlessly instead
Because she's so, so tiny and frail,
But she tilts her wee head at the sound of your
voice.
She's so adorable, you can hardly believe she's
yours.

You haven't left the NICU since the moment she was admitted.
The one nurse who doesn't seem to have a vendetta against you
Promises that it's normal to go home to shower, to breathe, that you have nothing to prove
But it's not about that.

You think if you were to leave her,
Your heart might just shatter.
And so you coo her name to her over and over,
Kiss her tiny fists when the staff aren't looking.

You whisper gentle reassurances into the incubator
Of the life she'll have with you if only she holds on,
If she can just be brave, fight on, for a few weeks longer.
And you promise her with all your heart that you'll never, ever hurt her again.

Statistics

People treat you differently, when they realise you're her mum.
You suppose it's only to be expected.
But still.
It hurts.

Perhaps it was naïve of you, but those first awful weeks sat beside your daughter's incubator,
Standing guard over her, overprotective mama bear,
You allowed yourself to believe that once she was discharged, it would get better.
That the outside world wouldn't regard you with the same disdain as did the NICU staff.

As it turns out, you were hilariously wrong.

When you and your mum take your baby out together, her pushing the pram
And you cradling her in your arms,
Strangers smile at you approvingly, see a big sister helping her mother with her youngest.
But the moment you venture out with her alone, everything changes.

It's always worse when you're in your school uniform, and that infuriates you,
Because it's not as though you're the only mum in the world to juggle a baby and a career.
Your career just happens to be getting through your Highers, then your Advanced Highers,
Then a degree.

That's what your own mum says, at least, when the guilt is overwhelming.

You hate the way you're stared at in public when it's just you and your wee best friend for life.
Your mum and your favourite teacher Miss McAlister and your support worker at the SARC
Tell you not to take it personally.
That everyone who matters knows you're doing an incredible job, so screw everyone else.

But that isn't the point, somehow.

You know what they're thinking.
The old ladies on the bus who tutted when they heard you refer to yourself as 'Mummy,'
The latest in your baby's long line of paediatricians
Who took one look at your band tour t shirt and your eyeliner and asked where her mother was.

The receptionist at the local swimming pool who said she was sorry,
But your daughter needed to be accompanied by an over-eighteen,
The middle-class kids at your new school who shout at you across the street,
And the disapproving parents of every single one of them you try to befriend.

You know exactly what they're all thinking.

For all the disapproval and downright snobbery and scorn with which the outside world regard you,
They stare at your daughter with sadness and sympathy.
Your beautiful wee daughter who's perpetually happy as long as she's in your arms-
And she's in your arms constantly, because it's hard enough putting her down when you're in school.

They stare at her as though they feel hopelessly sorry for her
Because in their eyes,
She's been saddled with an irresponsible, selfish, immature teenage mother
Who'll let her down again and again.

They don't seem to notice the way she looks at you.

She's the happiest baby you've ever known.
She always has been, as long as you're with her.
She babbles away to you contently in a language only she speaks, but somehow
You understand her perfectly.

She rests her head against your shoulder voluntarily the way only babies do,
And she's oblivious- oblivious to the stigmatisation the pair of you are subjected to,
Oblivious to the fact she has a seventeen-year-old, ex-junkie, former school dropout for her mother,
To all of it.

She just loves you.
You're her whole world, save for those six hours of the school day when her nana has her for you.
She's tiny, and she's helpless, and she depends on you for everything,
Trusts you unconditionally to feed her, comfort her, care for her, love her back.

That's what the strangers who shake their heads at you will never understand.

You love her more than you can even explain,
and you want the world for her.
You're painfully aware of the odds.
Social Services talked you through them when
she was barely a week old,
Told you she was more likely to leave school
with no qualifications, have her own baby by
fifteen.

Just because you're her mother.

They told you she's at an increased risk of
turning to drugs and alcohol herself,
Of struggling to form relationships as an adult,
A lifetime of poverty and unemployment… the
list went on.
They were trying to scare you, you suspect, and
it worked.

You're hypervigilant with her.
It's not that you love her more because you feel
you have to compensate
For your age and resulting incompetence-
You couldn't possibly love her any more than
you already do.

But you make absolutely sure to prove it to her.

You spend every single moment you possibly
can with her-
You come home from school and you complete
your homework with her in the baby sling,
Feel her wee heartbeat against your chest and
tell yourself it's alright.

That there's no reason to feel guilty.
That you're making sure she knows she's loved
and showing her the importance
Of getting an education at the same time,
Because you and your daughter will never, ever
be a statistic.

Separation Anxiety

You come so painfully close to dropping out
during your first term at university.
Not just once, either.
You contemplate dropping out multiple times a
day.

It's not the course.
That aspect of it all is everything you've
dreamed of for as long as you can remember.
Sometimes in your lectures, you have to pinch
yourself, because you can't quite believe you're
here.

It's not the other students on your corridor, or in
your lectures, or the squash society
You sign up to because you loved it at school,
Before you gave up your extra-curriculars and
your social life in the name of teenage
motherhood.

It's not the independence,
Or the halls of residence canteen,
Or the early starts for lectures and the long hours
spent at placement.

It’s leaving your two-year-old behind.
She cries down the phone to you every night for the first two weeks,
And your heart shatters each and every time, because it’s all your fault.

You’d planned to study at the university a ten-minute bus ride from home,
But your application was rejected.
And so you’re an hour and twenty-three minutes away in Dundee- not that you’re pedantic about it

Left your daughter with your mother- her idea,
Because she wanted you to have a chance to get a proper education and regain the freedom
You surrendered, build a better future for you and your wee ray of sunshine.

Because she is.
She’s your ray of sunshine.
You knew that already, but nothing confirmed it like leaving her behind.

When there’s seventy miles between you,
The ache in your heart is so overwhelming that it’s a battle just to remember how to breathe.

You cling on for your weekends back at home with her, for your mum bringing her down to visit.

It's the little things you miss.
You miss her wee hands pawing at your side when she's after your attention,
Tangling in your hair when she's tired, or anxious, or just plain clingy.

You miss your night-time snuggles, her small body pressed into your side
Because you've been sharing a bed at home-
There's no room for a toddler bed so when she outgrew her cot, she just came in with you instead.

You miss the way she sounds out 'Mummy' in the accent
Of the city you and your mum packed up and moved to for a fresh start after she left the NICU,
And wiping down her palms with baby wipes when she's dissected her lunch again.

You miss tearing after her along the beach when she makes a beeline for the North Sea in October,

Her kisses, her laughter, the feel of her hand in yours.
You miss her.

Everybody warned you being her mum was going to be the hardest thing you'd ever done,
When she was born.
But nobody said the hardest part would be to survive without her.

Selkie Shores

"Mummy!" she shouts, skips through the waves
blissfully as they lap against the sand,
Mermaid-scale swimsuit, hair a tangled mess
you'll be battling with the conditioning spray
later.
"Mummy, are you coming in? Mummy!"
"In a bit!" you call.
And you will.
You just want to watch her play a little longer
first.

It's the summer holidays at her nice,
middle-class primary school in its nice,
middle-class suburb,
And so naturally, as soon as you could book a
week off from your new, grown-up job
You bundled her into your batted, second-hand
Mazda Sedan and off you drove to Lewis-
Because your highlander and islander blood runs
deep, and it flows in her, too.
You crave the solitude.
You can savour her out here in a way you simply
can't back home.

She's growing up so fast.

You finished university at the start of summer,
graduation ceremony booked for next month
And getting yourself a degree was the right
decision- you aren't questioning that.
It was the right decision for both of you,
long-term. But just now…
You've been a part-time mum since she was two
years old, away for weeks at a time.
And it's not going to be like that anymore, but
you've missed out on so much already.

You baby her.
You know you do.
She tells you so.
Your mum tells you so, too,
But somehow,
It hits harder when it comes from your wee girl
herself.

You've been back to being her mother
twenty-four-seven for approximately three
weeks,
And in that time,
You've been bombarded with a constant stream
of
Mummy-I-can-do-it-myself,
Mummy-let-me-do-it, Mummy-I'm-not-a-baby.
That last one hits hardest, because of course
she's a baby.

She'll always be your baby.

You wish you could keep her tiny and dependent
and needy and safe with you forever,
But of course, it doesn't work that way.
She squeals in delight at the cold chill of the
inner seas against her skin,
And you know you're hopelessly biased, but
she's adorable.
Just the way her toes painted with your nail
polish curl into the sand in delight
Is enough to make your heart sing; ancient,
maternal, unconditional.

"Mummy!" she calls again. "Mummy, come
on!"
She throws herself happily into the waves, head
disappears beneath the surface
And it's only for a moment, but you bolt, run
towards her, protective mama bear.
"Don't do that!" you scald her as she laughs,
sunlight glistens against the ocean on her palms.
"Don't do what?" she asks, oh-so-innocent.
"You know what I mean! Your… I don't know!
Your mermaid impression…"

"I'm not a mermaid," she tells you, just a wee
touch of pretentiousness. "I'm a selkie."
God, she's your daughter.

You've carved her ancestry into her with all of the fire and determination you could muster,
Because that half of her that's you is the only one she has.
That, and the otherness within her scares you a little.
Not that she'll ever know.

"Selkies can get swept out, too!" you shout,
And if you were talking to anyone else,
You'd be saying that selkies are nothing but a folktale.
But she's yours.
And for her,
You'd believe in anything.

"I'm fine!"
"You're too far out!"
"I'm fine, Mummy!"
You roll your eyes, strip your coverup, run in after her.
You catch her in your arms, and she smells of saltwater, kids factor fifty plus,
The tropical twist ice lolly that melted halfway down her arm before she could finish it.

She laces her arms around your neck and your feet just about touch the ground,

So you move with the waves, half-jumping,
half-floating,
Effortless, because it's always effortless, when
you're with her.
"There!" she says triumphantly, points out into
the sea. "There's a selkie! There, Mummy!"
"It's a seal," you tell her.
"No, it's not!"

You're home.

Built-In Best Friend

She's eight years old when you start taking her to gigs.
It seems like the perfect solution.
As much as you don't miss being away from her
Those dark, dark days of part-time parenthood around the university holidays,
The one thing you do miss is the freedom you had to go out
When you didn't have to plan your social life around childcare.

That, and you're so haunted by guilt all evening when you do find a babysitter,
You can't relax anyway.
And so as soon as you feel she's just about old enough,
When a concert comes up you'd love to go to,
You just buy her a ticket
And off you both go together.

You figure one of the few advantages of having a seventeen-year age gap with your child
Must surely be that you'll like the same music,
But it doesn't quite work out that way.

She falls victim instead to the soft, melancholy
sounds of her ancestors-
Where she first encountered it, you never quite
establish.
Perhaps it's in her bones.

That said, she loves going with you.
And you love going with her.
She's the friend for life you didn't even know
you needed until you felt her first kick.
You suspect a large aspect of the appeal from her
perspective- coming with you, that is-
Is that because she feels as though she's your
best friend, too
And so you let her wear your makeup, buy her a
tour t shirt to match your own.

Inevitably it fits her like a dress, you tell
yourself it's absolutely not a waste of money,
Because by the time she's in high school she'll
have the coolest wardrobe going.
You make a show of letting her wear your
handbag with your phone and the house keys,
Tell her it's her job to look after you
And you're not really drunk, of course you're
not.
You'd never, ever get yourself drunk when
you're on mum duty, but it makes her feel
special.

You lift her into your arms when she's not quite tall enough to see the stage
And you dance with her, clasp her hand in yours as you wave along to the music,
Cover her ears when the lyrics get a wee bit explicit for your liking,
Or the look on her face tells you she's finding it all too loud.
You tell her how lucky you feel to have a best friend who'll come along with you to anything-
Because that's absolutely true.

She's at an age now at which she's starting to understand
That she doesn't have a normal mum, whatever that means.
She's beginning to notice how often her friends' parents assume you're her older sister,
The stares that follow you both down the supermarket aisles when she calls you Mummy.
It's only a matter of time before it dawns on her that you lack the life experience to guide her
That you would have possessed, if only you'd had her at a nice, sensible age.

But there's nothing you can do about that.
You can't change that she's stuck with a former teen mother,

And so you set out to embrace the advantages
instead.
The very thing that makes it difficult to know
how best to mother her at times
Is the reason you'll have a deeper connection
with her forever; you're certain of that.
After all, what's the point of having a baby in
high school if she can't be your built-in best
friend?

Homecoming

She’s ten years old, by the time you’ve scraped
together the money for a house deposit.
And even then, your mum and grandparents help
you out.

You’ve been desperately putting money aside for
a home of your own for you and your wee girl
Ever since you started your first job: one day a
week at the café round the corner from uni
That you didn’t need on top of your student loan,
took on purely to boost your savings account.
But even with that, it takes you a decade.

You were utterly determined that you’d move
into your own place when you graduated,
Just the two of you.
But the older she grows, the more money she
costs you-
And you don’t resent that, of course you don’t.

You go without new clothes for years so you can
shop for her instead, and before you know it
She’s halfway through primary school, scarily
grown-up and independent

and you find yourself forking out for figure
skating lessons, highland dancing, brownie
camp.
You sacrifice spending money on yourself
because you refuse to let your age negatively
impact her.

It takes you a little longer to build up your ISA
because you want to give her the childhood you
had,
With your two, married, financially stable and
old-enough-to-be-socially-acceptable parents.
That's what you're trying to say.
But finally, just after her tenth birthday, you
qualify for a mortgage.

And there's no doubt in your mind you would
have managed it years earlier had you not had
her,
But you wouldn't be without your wee shadow
for anything.

You take her to each and every house viewing as
your second opinion-
And you know full-well it would have been
more sensible to bring your mum along instead,
But it's your first home together, your family of
two.
It feels special.

She's off school for half-term the week you get the keys.
You make her unlock the front door the first time, all by herself,
Because you did it all for her- all of it, in its entirety.
You shudder to think where you might be now had the morning-after-pill worked its magic after all.

Ikea has never seemed as magical as it is the day you take her furniture shopping,
Pick her out a bed of her own, cloud-patterned duvet cover she's set her heart on.
You paint her bedroom walls her favourite colour with all the love and enthusiasm of a new mother;
It's taken you ten years, but finally, you can give her a bedroom of her own.

You feel so utterly triumphant that first night in your new home,
Tucking her under her own covers, kissing her goodnight, closing the door behind you.
But when you crawl into your own bed two hours later, lights on, no need to undress in the dark,
The mattress dips.

"You alright?" you whisper, stretch out your arms for her to cuddle into your side.
"Sweetheart?"
"Yeah," she replies sleepily, yawns, settles. "I just missed you."

Pieces of You

At your baby girl's primary school,
The other parents save for her friends' mums and dads view you
As the negligent, irresponsible former teen mother based purely on the fact
That in their eyes, you don't look old enough to have a child her age.
While in contrast, your daughter's teachers and the parents who actually know you
Say you're the textbook definition of an overprotective, helicopter mother.

You'd love to say that the truth is the absolute best of both contrasting impressions:
That you're a healthy mix of laid-back but attentive enough,
Mothering, not smothering, but deep down,
You know full well there's rather a lot of truth to the latter description of your parenting style.
Maybe it's because you missed out on weeks at a time of the toddler stage with her,
Her first two years of school, and all the growing up that came with that.

You don't know.

All you know is you find it so goddamned hard
to recognise when to let go, sometimes.
It possibly doesn't help that she's still so tiny.
All the way through primary school she's been
the smallest in her year-
Smaller than a good half of the year below, too,
as far as you can tell.
She'll be off to high school soon enough, and
that terrifies you.

It terrifies you because you know you should let
her walk there and back with her friends,
Shouldn't give in to your protective mummy
instincts screaming at you to accompany her
yourself,
But the truth is, you're afraid.
When she was born, her neonatologist warned
you it would take her a while
To catch up with her peers, but she'll be twelve
this year
And still there's no sign of it happening.

It would be so horribly easy for someone to
overpower her- you know that better than most.
How are you supposed to let her out of your
sight when you've borne the brunt of this
world's evils?
And you know you would think so, but the older
she gets

The more beautiful she becomes,
And that just makes it all worse.
You sign her up for self-defence classes at the local leisure centre, just in case.

The point is, you know you're overprotective.
Her friends' parents start inviting her to sleepovers when she's eight
But you turn them all down until she's eleven,
Because she just seems far too young to be away from you overnight.
(You know full-well that sounds ridiculous when you left her with your mother for university,
But in the years since you graduated, the idea of being apart from her has become unbearable.)

You'd miss her too much.
That's what it's really about.
You've been in your new house together long enough to call it home,
But she's still sleeping in your bed with you; an old habit neither of you want to break
And even if she'd be fine without you for a night or so,
You aren't sure you'd cope without her.

You know that's pathetic, but it's how you feel.
And so when she comes home with a permission form for the P7 camping trip

Babbling excitedly about three days of kayaking
and toasting marshmallows in the Black Isle,
You're torn.
You have to let her go sooner or later, your best
friend Fiona tells you- and you know she's right.
But all the same, that it's easy for her to say that
when her own daughter just turned three.

You let her go, in the end.
All the other parents are fine with letting their
children spend two nights in a cold, cramped
tent
Supervised by a grand total of six adults, she
tells you,
And she's so convinced she's going to be
missing out on the best week ever
That you don't have it in you to say no.
It's only two nights, you tell yourself, repeat it
like a mantra.

She's not used to sleeping without you any
longer and you're worried she'll find it
overwhelming,
So you write her wee notes to open each
morning when she wakes up, each night she
goes to sleep,
While she's gone.

Your own mum is horrified when you tell her, informs you that the other kids will tease her senseless,
But you pack them neatly into your daughter's camp holdall regardless.
When the coach drives away towards the A96, you're the only parent who cries.

The next fifty-six hours seem to last an utter lifetime.
You knew your life revolved around her, but you hadn't quite appreciated the true extent of it
Until she's gone, and you're home from work and there's no one to cook for,
No one to test on their spelling homework,
No one to cuddle up with on the sofa and make you feel needed, oh-so-loved.
It's different than being aware from her at university, somehow- because there was an end-goal, then.

One night without your wee shadow,
And you've no idea how your peers who did the sensible thing and didn't have a baby in high school
Fill their time.
You end up curled up under her favourite blanket, her guinea pig in your arms

And her favourite film on the TV just to feel close to her,
Until finally, it's time to collect her from the school playground.

"So did you miss Mummy at all?" you ask her hopefully, hold her hand as you walk home together.
Her holdall slung over your shoulder, and she frowns for a moment, contemplates.
"Ummmm…" she offers unapologetically, in the way only children can. "A little bit."
"Oh, thanks!" you protest. "I've had no one to heat up your nana's veggie haggis sausages for
Or fight for the TV remote, I've been lost all week!"
She giggles.

And then she stops.
"Did you carry on reading Northern Lights without me?" she asks urgently,
And you pause, just long enough to make her worry. "Mummy!"
"Would I dare?" you tease her, and she laughs, wraps her arms around your waist.
"Love you," she says, and at last, you can breathe again.
"Love you too."

Teenage Diaries

You spent so much of her time in primary school
worrying she wouldn't fit in because of you.
You weren't around for socialising at the school
gates during drop-off and pick-up
Most of her P1-3 years, could only involve
yourself in that aspect of your daughter's life
In your own university holidays,
Or the Fridays you'd be free of lectures and
tutorials and placements in the afternoons,
And so you'd run straight to the train station, be
home in time to surprise her in the playground.

The pure joy and excitement on her wee face
those days she wasn't expecting to see you there
Would melt your heart every single time.
She'd run over from the pupil entrance and
throw herself into your arms,
And you'd hug her tight and swing her round
and tell her how much you missed her.
The other mums and dads would smile
approvingly at first, assume you were her big
sister.
Then they'd hear her call you Mummy, and
everything would change.

You and your own mum couldn't help but notice
that after you'd done the school run a few times,
Your wee girl's birthday party invites started to
decline, playdates stopped being reciprocated
And you wouldn't have let it bother you, except
she noticed, too.
She was only five years old but already she was
being penalised
For something utterly out of her control,
And the worst of it was, it was all your fault.

It became painfully apparent within weeks of
your baby starting school
That she was the only child in her year born to a
teenage mother- the only one in the school,
possibly
Because it was that kind of area your mum
packed you both up to move to, after she was
born.
You worked out all-too quickly that you'd never
be accepted by the other parents-
The majority of them, at least,
Fought so hard to prove to them you were a
good mum despite your age, but it was never
enough.

By the time she was in P4 and you'd graduated
from university- back to being her full-time
mum again,

The way it should be- she had a close-knit group of friends,
And maybe it was because they knew your own mum, because you were living under her roof,
But their parents seemed to just about trust you with their children.
You'd spend hours cleaning the house from top to bottom when you had them over after school,
Cook the healthiest meals you knew how, set up all the outdoor activities, desperate for approval.

You felt as though you weren't just doing it for you, but for teen mums and their offspring everywhere.
Because you and your wee best friend from birth might be the only ones just now
In that middle-class suburb of the picturesque beachside city to which you just didn't quite belong,
But sooner or later, its inhabitants were bound to encounter others.
You wished they'd understand for you, for your child, for all those who'll inevitably come after you,
That your maternal capability is not and has never been dictated by your age.

As it turns out, though, you worried needlessly.
Well, you didn't.

Not completely.
You spent countless nights lying awake
worrying that teen mum snobbery
Was negatively impacting your daughter's
friendships- and you'd argue no part of that was
needless, Because your wee ray of sunshine
deserves the world.

Navigating primary school friendships and the
inevitable power of parental veto was a constant
worry-
There's no getting around that.
You can't deny there were nights when you
broke down and cried because you felt so
horribly guilty,
Wanted to scream, tell the other parents that you
didn't exactly plan to become a mum at
seventeen,
That it could quite easily have been them.
But when she reaches high school, thankfully,
it's different.

Your experience as mum to a high schooler is
wonderfully, refreshingly different,
Because what the other parents think of your
situation starts to matter less and less.
Teenagers make their own decisions as to who
they spend their time with.
You should have realised that.

You know it better than most, after all.
That's how you got pregnant in the first place.

By the time your daughter is in S2, newly a teenager, the tables have turned,
And it's your house her friends are happily flocking to after school.
You can't take all the credit, obviously.
That your baby ends with such a wonderful group of friends by the time she's thirteen
Is a testament to her gentle nature, her loyalty, her ability to make just about anybody
Feel as if they've known her forever, breeze into their lives as though she's been there all along.

She would have been popular enough regardless,
You don't doubt that.
But you can't deny that once she's in high school,
The fact that her friends see you as the young, cool mum
They wish they had themselves
Certainly helps matters.

You seem to become the person they turn to when they're in trouble, somehow.
You can't quite pinpoint when exactly during your wee girl's high school career it begins.

But somewhere along the way, you become the adult in her friends' lives that they'll open up to
When they've done something stupid,
When they've played at being grown and found out the hard way they aren't quite ready to fly alone,
When they're craving their own mother's comfort, but they're too frightened to confess.

You never quite work out whether they'll confide in you,
Let you be the one to guide them over their own parents, their own teachers,
All the other arguably more logical fixtures in their lives,
Because the mere seventeen years between you and them renders you more relatable,
Or because your biggest supporter has sung your praises as non-judgemental adult to be trusted,
Or whether it's because they figure you became a mum in high school; you've been there, done it all.

Whatever the reason, you don't mind.
You quite like teenagers- you chose to educate them for a living, after all.
You feel a sense of maternal responsibility, of loyalty, to teenagers.

You wouldn't change your own teenager for the world- not one thing about her,
But your heart is heavy with the guilt of the NICU stay she endured, the complications, the damage
Inflicted upon her because as a teenager yourself, you had no one you felt able to turn to.

And so when she brings home a friend with boyfriend trouble,
Or the weight of the world upon their shoulders, or god forbid, a pregnancy scare,
You'll hold them in your arms like they're your own,
Promise them they'll be alright, that the world will go on turning.
You'll console them like you wish someone had consoled you all those years ago,
Try your hardest to convince them to tell their parents, do-what-I-say, not-what-I-do.

And when you've waved them off from the doorstep-
Or settled them onto the blow-up mattress, if they won't go home,
Because you've slept in enough squats in your time and you won't have them go through that, too-

You look at your own child, thank a god you
only began believing in again when he brought
you her
That she's still so open with you, truly believes
you when you promise her she can tell you
anything.
The joke's on the other,
actually-old-enough-to-be-parents after all.

Conviction

You'd never intended for her to find out that way.
You'd never really thought about how you'd eventually tell her-
And that's your failing as her mother, you recognise that.
But you certainly never intended for her to find out the way she does.

You should have told her sooner, you curse yourself,
Sat beside her at the kitchen table.
You should have told her much, much sooner,
because now her father's eyes are pleading with you-
Her father's eyes but not, because she'll never be his.

You always knew you'd have to tell her one day.
She deserves to know; it wouldn't have been fair to keep it from her forever.
You knew you'd have to tell her, but still you pushed it far, far out of your mind

Told yourself that she was still too young,
because you were afraid the truth would break
her.

You've left it far too late.
She's shaking.
You've arrived home from work to find her
trembling violently, newspaper spread out over
the table,
And when you crouch beside her, ask what's
happened, she points to the mugshot on the front
page.

"Is he my dad?" she whispers.
She sounds utterly, painfully broken.
You reach for the newspaper pages, ready to ask
her what on earth put that idea into her head,
But instead, your eyes lock with his.

Your heart stops, because suddenly, you're
seventeen years old again.
You're seventeen years old and he's up in your
face, venomous, raging,
And his fist slams into your stomach, leaves you
winded,
But it's his cruel taunts that sting.

You haven't seen him since the day you ran.

You finally mustered the courage to leave him behind for good
When your beautiful, kind, perfect daughter made her presence known,
And you knew you had to get yourself out,.

You've always known.
It's been painfully clear since the day your gorgeous wee girl was born,
But you only realise the extent of it as his features scowl at you from the pages of a newspaper,
Angrier, viler, than his gentle double quivering at your kitchen table could ever be.

You can't lie to her.
She already knows; you can see it in her eyes.
And so you take her hand in yours, cup her cheek, nod gently, controlled, in confirmation.
She crumbles.

In those next few moments, she seems to forget how to breathe.
She sobs and sobs until her breath catches alarmingly in her throat,
Comes in panicky, incomplete gasps and you pull her into your arms, clutch her to your chest

And pray with all your might that the beating of your heart against hers will remind her what to do.

You're lost.
You don't know how to comfort her, make it go away-
Because you can't make it go away; you know that only too well.
Nothing can.

And so you just hold her, instead.
"I love you," you whisper in her ear, over and over.
"It's okay."
"I love you, so, so much. You're okay."

At last her breathing levels out a little,
And she pulls away, looks right into your eyes and her own plead with you to be honest with her.
"Did he hurt you, too?" she asks.
Deep down, you suspect she already knows the answer.

"Have you read it all?" you realise, nausea building within you.
All of a sudden, you realise her innocence is gone, robbed from her forever

And there's nothing you can do to claim it back.
"The whole article?"
"Mum…" she begs.

You shudder.
You haven't the time to scan the pages, not now; you'll do that when she's in bed.
You don't know for sure what horrors they contain, but monsters like him don't change.
You can guess.

"… Yes," you admit softly. "Yes. That's why I got out, when I realised I was pregnant with you."
She bursts into tears.
You hug her so tightly that her ribs dig into yours, squeeze her, but she just cries and cries.
"I'm sorry, Mum," she sobs. "I'm so, so sorry."

All You Wish She Knew

Everything changes, the day she finds out.
You hate yourself for that.
You've spent her whole life trying to gently prepare her-
Because deep down, you always knew you couldn't protect her forever.

It was easier, when she was wee.
Those awful few months after she discovers the truth about her father
You desperately wish she could be your wee baby again,
Because the issue of her paternity couldn't have mattered less when her entire world was you.

You know she's wondered for a long time-
because she's noticed, of course she has.
She's noticed that her friends, her classmates, the whole goddamned world has a father-
Or at least knows why they don't have a father, has an origin story, an explanation.
You could never give her that.

You were always determined you would never lie to her.
You wouldn't take your grandmother's advice and conjure up a romantic tragedy to protect her,
Because if ever she did discover the truth, that would make it all worse.
And it's just DNA.

That's what you've always told yourself, and it's what you tell her, now,
When she's distraught, sobbing to you desperately that she's a monster by association,
Can't seem to separate herself from the sleekit bastard in the newspapers serving a life sentence.
She might be half him from a genetic perspective, but she's half you, too.

It's just DNA.
She's almost grown, now, and in the sixteen years you've been blessed with being her mother,
Not once have you seen even the faintest trace of her so-called father's cruel violence within her.
His DNA might have combined with yours to give her life, but that's where her connection to him ends.

You wish she could see it like you do.
You wish she realised that the physical resemblance she bears to that half of her ancestry is irrelevant,
That he might be genetically her father, but he'll never be her dad.
And you tried so hard to instil that in her right from the start, but clearly, you failed.

She'd just started P1 the first time she brought it up.
She asked you where her daddy was
During one of your nightly phone calls home from uni to read her a bedtime story,
And calmly, controlled, you told her she didn't have a dad, because that's how you've always seen it.

You've stuck by that ever since.
You've always tried to ensure that she never feels the absence of a father figure in her life,
To strengthen her sense of the Scottish heritage that flows in her veins from you,
Emphasise beyond all doubt that she's your daughter, your history, all you.

You tried so goddamned hard, but clearly, it wasn't enough.
You're learning that the hard way now,

Because the truth has shattered her.
And you just can't seem to make it better.

You're watching her fade away- and not just physically, either.
Though you're out of your mind with worry over that, too.
Her appetite seems to disappear the moment she's confronted with the other half of her parentage.
Mealtimes become a painful battle you know you can't afford to lose, but she just won't eat.

Part of you wants to put a stop to her rigorous cross country training regime,
Cut back on her dance classes, because maternal instinct is screaming at you
That she's overexercising on top of the eating disorder unfolding before your eyes.
The trouble is, those seem to be the only things that make her happy.

You don't know if you should be more alarmed about the weight she's lost
Or the defeated, lifeless look in her eyes;
You bounce alarmingly from one to the other and back again- until, that is,
You discover the bloody tissue in the bathroom bin, dismantled razer heads.

Because that's the worst.
You've never felt as utterly helpless as you do that night.
"I love you," you whisper in her ear over and over, cuddle her close to your chest.
"I know," she whispers back, voice trembling.
"But I don't understand how."

Sometimes, she allows herself to break down in front of you
And as strange as it sounds, you're relieved when she does.
The rest of the time, she seems so horribly numb, and you worry constantly
That she's so afraid of upsetting you, she's bottling it all up inside.

She tells you there's a tight feeling in her chest that she can't shake,
An invisible chokehold around her neck,
And before you know it, you're watching helpless as she sobs harder and harder
Breath catches in her throat and she's hyperventilating, terrified, lost inside her head.

You don't know how to help her.
You just don't know how to help her, and you curse yourself,

Because a part of you wonders if the age gap has finally caught up with you both,
Whether you simply lack the life experience and the maturity and the wisdom to take her pain away.

If only she understood how much she means to you.
If only she could see that she's your everything;
In a way, you hate that expression, because it's so painfully overused that
It's mere empty words, now- but it's true.

She saved you.
You've told her that countless times over the years,
But you're not sure if she believes you,
If she truly appreciates just how much of a mess you were in, before she came along.

Had it not been for those two red lines on a plastic stick
That you may or may not have stolen from the pharmacy on Kenmure Street,
You'd be sleeping rough, by now, still stuck in that abusive relationship from which she came,
Off your face on crack and booze and god only knows what else to take the edge off it all.

You know you would.
You know it because you'd stopped caring about yourself a long time ago,
When that test confirmed your suspicions.
You didn't care about you, but you cared about her more than you can even explain.

You wish you could help her see she's everything you ever wanted-
Even though she was everything you'd ever wanted to avoid, too.
You never wanted to depict it all as a love letter to teenage motherhood
Because you want better for her, but that doesn't mean she wasn't exactly what you needed.

You wish she realised that you feel at peace with yourself when you're with her
In a way you never have with anyone else,
That just the way she looks at you, even now, sixteen years old
Makes you feel loved, and needed, and wonderfully safe, somehow.

She makes you feel safe because when you're with her,
You're brave enough to defend you both from any threat imaginable.

Because no matter how old she grows, she'll always be your wee baby,
And the protective mama bear instinct you feel for her is unrivalled still, unwavering.

You wish she knew how proud she makes you.
She's the same age now that you were when you got pregnant,
And you've joked with her that if she finishes school without making you a grandmother,
Without an off-the-rails phase, you'll have done your job right.

You've told her over and over that she's the best thing you ever did,
But you're not sure she believed you even before.
Still, though, she is.
She fills your heart with something warm and fuzzy you can't quite articulate.

You wish she believed that she's been your best friend since she was born-
Since before she was born, even,
Because you've had her to hold on for at your absolute lowest,
And time and time again, she's helped you see the sun again.

That your home is with her, wherever she goes,
That it always will be.
That a part of you truly believes she was this universe's divine gift to you,
Because every inch of her completes you like no one else can.

You wish she could see that the distress she's in now,
The pain that the truth about her paternity has caused her hurts you, too-
Unbearably so.
But you wouldn't change it for the world.

You wouldn't change who her father is,
Because if she wasn't half him, then she wouldn't be her,
And you love her, every inch of her, exactly as she is.
That's all you wish she knew.

You can tell her, of course- and you do.
You tell her all of that over and over, but you know she doesn't believe you.
And so you fuss over her as though she's a little younger than her sixteen years-
Except you're told constantly you baby her anyway, so perhaps it's more like a lot.

You cuddle her a little more, tell her you love her more,
Resort to a love language of constant physical contact
Because she doesn't seem to believe your gentle reassurances,
So you desperately hope your touch might drill it into her.

You hold her in your arms whenever she'll let you,
Her heartbeat against yours reassuring you a little
Because she's so painfully thin, frail,
That you're afraid she might just snap.

You hug her tightly, stroke her hair,
Tell her she's beautiful and you're stupidly jealous
Because you are, and you've a horrible feeling all she sees now when she looks in the mirror
Is everything she's afraid she is- everything you know she'll never, ever be.

And on days when that doesn't work, either, you phone in sick to work,
Phone her in sick to school, curl up on the sofa with her and just hold her, helpless.

"It's going to be alright, sweetheart," you
whisper in her ear,
Breathe in her scent as though she's your
newborn again.

"You're going to be alright."

Tha Gràdh Agam Ort

"This is the last time we're doing this, okay?
You need to get some sleep."
You're worried about the dark circles under her eyes.
You know she hasn't been sleeping.
You've been borderline obsessive about having her in bed by ten at the absolute latest
Ever since she started S5, because you're convinced her precarious mental state
Is a lot less precarious when she's getting her nine hours.

"Once I know all of these," she tells you, uncompromising.
She's undeniably your daughter.
You were like this, too; that's exactly why you worry about her.
You worked yourself to the point of exhaustion during your own Highers exams-
But that was because you were doing it all with her, eleven months old and stupidly clingy.

You near burnt yourself out at her age so she wouldn't have to.

"You do know all of these," you point out gently. "I know you do."
"I don't."
"You do. One more time, alright?" you bargain with her. "You'll see."
"Okay." She bites her lip, unconvinced, and you just want to hug her.
You just want to abandon her neatly drawn-up flashcards on the coffee table,
Pull her into your arms and tell her how brilliant she is, that she's going to do just fine.

You'd do it in a heartbeat if you thought it might help her,
But you know her too well.
She's the worst perfectionist you've ever known,
Chastises herself at the slightest error,
And you wish she'd treat herself with the kindness
She bestows on everyone around her.

Priorities, you tell yourself.
You've got the whole of her summer break in which to continue your desperate fight
To instil in her at least some vague sense of self-love and worth,

Her S6 year after that to ensure she's ready to fly the nest-
Because as much as you're afraid she won't be ready, you know you can't stop her.
You can worry about all of that once you've got her through her Highers exams.

"Mum."
"Alright!" you pacify her. "Alright, I'm just looking for some we haven't done yet. Dùthaich."
"Country," she translates, doesn't miss a beat, and you're so, so proud of her.
The language of your ancestors is a mystery to you, but in her gentle lilt, it seems effortless.
"Yep. Trioblaid."
"Problem."

"Co-dhùnadh."
"Decide."
"Meadhan."
"Centre."
"Thìr."
"Continent."

"What on earth are you worried about?" you ask her gently, trying to reassure her,
But she shakes her head, wraps her arms around herself protectively.

She's lost weight again.
You try to reassure yourself that she did her Nationals exams
Caught in the midsts of a full-blown eating disorder,
And she nailed those.

"Alright," you sigh. "Alright, we can do a few more, then. Atharrachadh clìomaid."
"Climate change." She laces her fingers together over and over, fidgets, radiates anxiety.
"There you go, you've got this. In-imrich."
"Immigration."
"Àiteachas."
"Agriculture."

You pause, close your eyes in concentration.
"Tha gràdh agam ort," you offer,
And she rolls her eyes at you, but still, she smiles.
"That's not on the flashcards, Mum."
"So?" you protest. "Tha gràdh agam ort," you tell her again, reach for her hand,
Hold it gently in yours and she leans into your arms, closes her eyes, calm at last.
"Love you too, Mum," she says. "An còmhnaidh.*"

*Always

Separation Anxiety II

You cry yourself to sleep every night, the first
week after you drop her off at university.
It's something of a full-circle moment,
Because you cried yourselves to sleep the first
week you left her behind for university yourself
All those years ago, and you desperately hope
she hasn't cried herself to sleep this time, too.

It's different this time round, of course.
That's what you tell yourself when the house
feels cold and empty,
When there's no one to cuddle up with during
your River City catch-up,
And you're accidentally making her a cup of tea
every time the kettle boils.

It's different this time- for her, at least,
Because she wasn't ready to be apart from you,
before, but she is, now.
It's her decision, this time, and that makes it
different.

It's different for her, but for you, the heartbreak
is undeniably the same.

You miss her so much already.
She's 3 whole hours away- and you suppose it
could have been worse,
That at least the promise of tuition-fee-free study
was enough to keep her in Scotland.
But that 3 hours, that 136 miles, is still the
greatest distance there's ever been between you.

It doesn't help that she's still such a constant
worry.
You were never going to find it easy to let her
go- you accept that.
But the more you read about how eating
disorders can thrive in university halls of
residence,
The more convinced you become that it's
different, for you and her.

She's been better, this past year.
She's been eating properly, getting enough sleep,
allowing herself some time off to actually relax
And her panicky, stress-induced meltdowns
seem to have gradually subsided as a result.
But veterinary school isn't exactly known for
being a low-pressure environment.

You worried about her so goddamned much as it was, when she was still at home with you.
She's going to have the most amazing time- you do know that.
You've been convinced she'd end up working with animals ever since she was wee;
She was charming the sheep on your grandparents' farm by the time she was eighteen months old.

She began begging you for a puppy almost the moment she could talk,
And every cat, every horse, every bloody highland cow she's ever encountered
Seems to instantly accept her as one of their own,
So all things considered, you think she's going to be just fine.

Just as long as she remembers she can call you whenever she's doubting herself,
Whenever she's struggling,
Whenever the workload feels like too much and she's afraid she can't do it,
Because you'll always be here to gently reassure her that she absolutely can.

She'll be alright, you tell yourself over and over,
Repeat it like a mantra.

She'll be alright.
You'll make sure of it.

Your friends think you're completely crazy,
when you admit you're pining after her.
You should be out celebrating, as far as they're
concerned.
You can finally experience the freedom you've
been waiting for your entire adult life;
You were a mother before you could even buy a
legal pint, but now, it's your time.

Except you don't want it to be your time.
Sometimes, just sometimes, when you'd have to
turn down a night out
Because you couldn't afford a babysitter, you'd
dream of this day.
But now it's here, you just want your baby back.

You take to wearing the sherpa hoodie she left
behind around the house, that first week
Because all of a sudden, autumn seems to have
set in.
That, and it smells of her,
Until you've worn it too much, and then it just
smells like you.

Is that pathetic?
You think it probably is.

You wonder if it would be even more pathetic to message and ask if she fancies a facetime chat,
Admit that her text updates aren't enough to heal the aching in your heart.

She sounds happy enough, in her messages,
Those windows into her new life that light up your phone like winter sunrise on Islay.
She's made a friend on her corridor, joined the highland dance society, settling in just fine.
Thank goodness.

You've tried so hard to keep from her just how heartbroken you are at her departure,
But somehow, she seems to know.
She keeps asking you how you are, in your text conversations.
You tell her you're fine, because you won't have her worrying.

You'd never admit it, but you've taken to crossing off the days on the kitchen calendar,
Counting down until she's home for the Christmas holidays.
You're secretly hoping you'll see her before then,
But you'd never, ever tell her so.

You never doubted that you made the right
decision- keeping her, that is.
But it's only once your house is cold and empty
That you start to wonder if maybe, just maybe,
You were always meant to be a teen mum.

You don't know how to function without her.
You'll learn, you know you will.
You'll do it for her, because you never want to
hold her back.
But god, you miss her.

You just miss her.
You miss her more than you even understand
yourself.
Your adult identity is so intrinsically woven
within your role as her mother,
That you're not entirely sure you know who you
are when she's not with you.

And so when she finally calls at the end of her
first week,
Tells you that everything's fine- she just misses
you,
Asks you how you make your veggie haggis
sausage rolls,
Your heart swells with relief.

Because she still needs you.

She still needs you,
And you still need her, too.
You think you always will.

Growing Pains

"You okay?"
"Yeah."
"You cold?"
"Only a wee bit."
"Are you shivering?"
She shifts awkwardly, never was any good at lying to you. "No."

"Yes you are," you insist. "You want me to…"
"Stop fussing, Mum," she protests,
And she's gone all-out
I'm-not-a-baby-anymore-Mummy,
Despite the fact that she's twenty years old and sharing your bed.

"I'm not fussing!"
"You are!"
"Alright! Alright, fine… oh my god, your feet are freezing…"
"They aren't!"
"They are! I'm sure you've got some thermal socks here you didn't take to uni. Shall I go and…"
"I'll be fine in a minute, Mum."

"If you're sure." Gently, you pull her into your arms, breathe her in.
She smells like the cherry blossom shower gel you picked up from the new spa shop in town
When she told you she was coming home this weekend
Mixed with just the faintest trace of the cigarettes you keep meaning to give up.

"I'll warm up in a minute," she tells you, curls into your side.
"Okay. Shall I put the light off?"
"Yeah."
You flip the switch on your bedside lamp. "You tired?"
"Uh huh."
"I'm not surprised. You've had a busy week…"

"It's been okay."
"Is that all your assignments done for the semester, then?"
"Just one the week after next."
"And then I get you home for Christmas break?" you ask hopefully.

You should count yourself lucky, really.
None of her schoolfriends seem to come home during term-time.

Meanwhile, your wee girl texted you last night to say
She was going to take the train home after her last lecture for the week,
And you had the afternoon off anyway,
So you jumped in the car and drove down to get her yourself instead.

She shifts, pulls the duvet up to her shoulders as though she absolutely is freezing cold after all,
And she's pressed up against you, your limbs tangled together, and so she cocoons you, too.
"I might stay in Edinburgh with Sorcha and Kirsty for a few days," she confesses. "Is that okay?"
You comb your fingers through her hair absentmindedly, savouring her.

"You do realise you don't have to ask me that, don't you?"
"I know. Is it okay, though?"
"Of course it is. I just want you to be happy, sweetheart," you tell her sincerely.
"Awww."
"You sure you're okay?"
She shrugs in your arms. "Why wouldn't I be?"

You pause.

"You haven't come home because you're struggling a bit?" you try, careful, casual as you can manage.
God, you worry about her.
She's in her third year of university now, thriving, and you're so, so proud of her.

But you can't help but worry she's a little more delicate than her peers,
A little more fragile,
A little more in need of your gentle reassurance than most twenty-year-olds.
But that's fine.
If she needs you like this forever, then that's just fine,
Because you know you'll need her forever, too.

She shakes her head, and you can breathe again.
"No," she says simply- sincerely, thank goodness. "No. I just missed you."
You smile, hug her tighter. "That's sweet."
She sighs softly, sinks into the mattress, and you know sleep is about to claim her.

"I love you."
"I love you more."
"I love you more."
"Stop. You've no idea how much you mean to me..."

"You stop…"
"No!"

You hardly ever get sentimental with her.
Not like this, at least.
But every now and then, you feel the need to tell her exactly what she means to you.
You never want her to think the word 'unwanted' belongs anywhere near your teenage pregnancy.

"I love you so much," you tell her quietly,
Stroke her cheek,
Momentarily allow yourself to forget she's twenty, not two. "I love you so, so much.
You saved me. You know that?"
"I know."
"I know, but I mean it."

She lets out a gentle, content yawn, grip on you loosens and you don't care how old she grows,
She'll always be your baby.
"I don't even want to think about where I'd be now if I hadn't had you," you admit.
"You're the best thing that ever happened to me.
You came out of the worst. But you were the best."

"… You aren't supposed to promote underage pregnancy, Mum," she slurs, fighting sleep.
"I'm not promoting it! I'm just saying… I wouldn't be without you. Not for anything. Ever."
Her breathing levels out, and you know she's asleep.
"This is exactly why they won't let me do the teen pregnancy talk for the S3s at work," you confess,
Even though you know come morning, she won't remember a word.
"I think I was always meant to have you. I needed a purpose, and then I had you."

Her horrible cold feet press up against your calves,
And you shudder, at first,
Roll your eyes.
But you wouldn't have her any other way.

Wherever You Will Go

The harsh chill of the North sea cleanses you.
It's Hogmanay, and the beach stretch a mere five minutes from home
Would inevitably have been deserted,
But you've driven out to Balmeadie regardless.

It's… magical, out here.
When winter sunrise hits the sand dunes
They seem to glow
With all of the warmth of your homeland that lingers even after summer has faded away.

You're a little more sentimental about it all today,
Because in your heart, you've made your decision.
If it's what your daughter wants, then it's what you want, too.
Your daughter whose lips are already blue tinged after all of ninety seconds.

Rolling your eyes, you grab her hand, run out with her right beside you-
You never go deep enough in winter that your feet can't touch the sand.
That isn't what this is about, for you two.
Well, for you, at least.

You keep your wild swimming regime up through winter
Because it invigorates you, somehow.
The bitter cold of the sea air in your lungs, saltwater against your skin reminds you
That you're imperfectly, wonderfully alive, keeps you from hibernating through the harsh winters.

And she comes along with you, your wee shadow,
Because as much as she complains she can't hack it in winter,
Longs desperately for Scottish sun and twenty degrees when she throws herself into these waters
Deep down, this is woven into the very strands of her DNA just like it is yours.

She's an islander.
She's an islander because you are, because your mother is, too,

Because you can trace her heritage all the way back to Islay-
And who cares about her other side?

Hand in hand, you run out of the waves and back up the beach together,
Laughing and shivering and screaming at the temperature contrast all at once,
That obnoxious best-friends-and-utterly-unbothered-by-how-annoying-you're-being energy,
As if it's just you and her, not merely on this beach, but in the whole of Scotland, the whole world.

Reaching your discarded bags, you spring into action,
Throw her stupidly overpriced fleecy changing robe… thing over her shoulders,
And once you're both dry,
You throw your own stupidly overpriced fleecy changing robe thing around her, too.

You're stupidly overprotective at the best of times- you know that-
But your innate mama bear tendencies come out in full force when you're worried she's too cold.
She's half Scottish, half hardened Hebridean sheep farmer, in her bones, and yet

Her lack of ability to regulate her own body
temperature scares you senseless, sometimes.

"Mum!" she protests, when you press the flask
of hot chocolate into her hands,
Adamant she's having the first sip. "Mum, I'm
fine."
"Your circulation's not normal," you worry, fight
against impossibly cold feet
To kick off your swim boots, shove your feet
back into your trainers.

"It's fine…"
"Your teeth are chattering," you point out,
utterly uncompromising.
You place one hand against her back as you
guide her back up the beach towards the car,
Maternal instinct urging you to get her into the
warm. "Come on."

"You're the one who drags me out here every
weekend."
"You enjoy it really."
"That's not the point! If you're that worried
about me freezing to death…"
"I'm not worried about you freezing to death,"
you lie. "I'd just rather get you straight in the
car…"

"With the heating on?"
"Exactly!"
"Doesn't that kind of defeat the object, though?" she argues.
"Aren't we supposed to take our time? You know, for the whole zen effect? Enjoy the sunrise?"

"In summer," you shrug. "In winter, I think just the cold-water benefits will do."
"Did you read that on your wild swimming forum thing?"
"Maybe. Did that help, though?" you ask, Watch her face carefully for clues to the status of her inner turmoil this morning.

"Hmm?" she feigns innocence, but you can see right through her.
You pull the car keys from your bag, unlock the doors, usher her into the passenger seat.
"You know what I mean. Did the swim clear your head a wee bit?"
She tenses, pulls her knees up to her chest on the passenger seat.

"I don't know," she confesses, bites her lip, torn.
"I just don't know what to do, Mum."
Her shivering is just about subsiding, but she looks so horribly lost.

You were up with her into the early hours debating it all,
Went back and forth a thousand times over and she's still apparently no further forward.

"Okay," you tell her calmly, turn the heating onto full. "Okay. What are you thinking this morning?"
"Honestly?"
"Yeah."
"That it's too far."

"It's only Newcastle," you remind her gently.
"It's not… I don't know. Exeter…"
"It's still England, though."
"You're so my daughter. Seriously, though," you point out gently. "It's only Newcastle. That's only a couple of hours from where you are right now…"

"It's two and a half hours from Edinburgh, actually."
"There you go, then…"
"But I'm already two and a half hours away when I'm in Edinburgh."
"So you're thinking no, then?"

"Yes… No… I don't know…"
She's radiating panic.

The weight of the decision before her seems to be eating her up inside, now,
And you wish you could make it for her, but even you know it doesn't work like that."

"You don't have to decide just yet, sweetheart. Do you? If they're giving you a week…"
"I don't know if I'm going to know in a week, though…"
"Then you can just say no," you tell her firmly. "If it doesn't feel right, you can just say no."
"I can't…"

"Of course you can. You've still got a whole semester of uni to finish…"
"I know…"
"So you've got plenty of time to apply for other jobs. Other jobs up here, if that's what you want…"
"Is that really pathetic, though…"

"No," you promise. "No, it's not. I didn't move away when I finished uni…"
"You had me, though. That's different."
"No, it's not. I could have moved away with you, if I'd wanted to. People do."
"I know."

She's so like you.

You don't always see it.
But when she's struggling like this, channelling your own indecisive energy
And reluctant to let anyone in, she's so painfully like you that you want to hold onto her forever.

Perhaps she might just let you.
"Alright," you try, adopting a new approach.
"You were telling me pros and cons last night…"
"Yeah."
"So they haven't changed?"

"Kind of."
"Okay…"
She sighs softly. "It's basically my dream job."
"Yep. Yep, I'd agree with that."

"And I'm probably not going to find anything else like it, am I?"
"You might…"
"I won't, Mum. Anywhere else, I'd have to choose between small animals and…"
"They can't be the only place that…"

"There aren't many roles like this for newly-qualified vets, though."

"Got you. You'd be fine in Newcastle, sweetheart," you reassure her gently. "You really would…"
"I know."
She fidgets, agitated.

"But?" you press.
"But what?"
"You don't sound too convinced…"
"I know I'd be fine in Newcastle," she confesses, quiet, ashamed. "I'd just really miss you."

Your heart melts.
You suspected as much.
You almost didn't allow yourself to believe it, before,
Thought you were seeing what you wanted to.

That sounds so selfish.
Your heart has been heavy at the thought of her moving so far away
Ever since she told you about her job offer,
And you fought so hard to keep your feelings a secret so she wouldn't feel obliged to stay.

But if she feels the same way you do…
"Okay," you begin carefully, take her hand in yours again. "Okay. This might sound crazy…"

"Yeah…"
"Well, I wasn't going to say it. But I'd really miss you, too. So what if…"

You take a deep breath.
You're terrified of her rejection,
Even though in your heart,
You know exactly what she'll say.

"What if I come with you?" you suggest.
She's silent for several moments.
"Would you want to, though?" she asks at last.
There's an air of peace about her being that wasn't there before.

"I'm open to it."
"Your home's here, though, Mum," she worries, and gently, you laugh, squeeze her hand.
"No, it's not," you tell her, and you don't care how embarrassingly sentimental you sound.
"My home's wherever you are."

Màthair

She throws you a surprise party for your fortieth birthday.
Well, you say surprise, except it's not a surprise- not really,
Because you've always been able to see right through her when she's trying to keep a secret.
You can see into her very soul, when it's about you.

You pretend you had no idea, of course.
You feign obliviousness when she tells you she's coming home for the weekend
Even though she'll be back for Easter break the week after,
And you've already told her you don't mind celebrating your birthday a few days late.

When you try to make plans for the weekend, she teeters,
Tries to encourage you to just go with the flow,
And so when your work friends turn down your proposal of a night out on Saturday,
Glance between each other shiftily, you're suspicious.

It's your own mum who finally gives the game away.
"I don't think she'll to want to go to Tollohill Wood on Saturday afternoon," she confesses
When you reveal your proposal you'll put to your daughter when she's home.
"I think she'll be setting up for…"

She catches herself just in time, but it's far too late.
The damage is already done, but you don't mind- it makes you smile, more than anything.
Your mum never was the best at keeping secrets.
It's one of the many reasons you didn't tell her you were pregnant until your waters broke.

Whether or not she confesses to your daughter that she's given the game away prematurely,
You don't know, but your wee girl goes all-out with the surprise element regardless.
She tells you she's taking you to the Pizza Express on Summer Street, when it's time to leave,
And you play along with her willingly, because you're not quite over the lengths she's gone to.

You're so, so lucky to have her.

That sounds horribly cliché, the kind of thing
any mother would say about their child, but it's
true.
She came into your life right when you needed
her as though she was always meant to be,
And ever since then, you've never needed a best
friend, because the vacancy was already filled.

She knows you better than you know yourself-
and that's cliché, too, but it's equally true.
She's hired the community hall to throw you a
ceilidh,
Gathered together your friends from work, from
the school you did your probation year at,
Your running group, even managed to get your
grandparents down from Islay.

(You'll laugh, when the food arrives at seven,
Because you'd assumed Pizza Express was a
cover story,
But as it turns out, she's ordered in takeaway,
knows better than to joke about doughballs.
You've taught her well.)

It's not just for your fortieth, she tells you-
So you can't complain. (Not that you ever
would, when she did it all for you.)
It's a farewell party, too, so you can celebrate
with your friends up here,

Because when she graduates in July, you'll both be off to Newcastle.

You've taken the plunge, accepted an offer on your house,
Found a new job at a North Shields secondary and god help you getting to grips with the curriculum,
But she's so, so excited to start her veterinary career, and that's all that matters.
For tonight, though, you're not worrying about any of that.

Everything about it is perfect- the party she throws you, that is.
You aren't always keen on being the centre of attention-
You put it down to teenage motherhood, because for so many years of her life
You were the centre of attention for all the wrong reasons.

But she seems to understand that, too.
She plans the whole thing perfectly.
The music and the dancing mean there's a constant distraction,
And you can weave your way through your friends and family all in one place to your heart's content.

Mostly, though, you just spend the evening
dancing with her.
Everyone else is here to celebrate your fortieth,
But you're celebrating your beautiful daughter.
Because against the odds, you did it- both of
you, together.

Somehow, you've succeeded in raising the
kindest, most intelligent,
Brave, selfless young woman you know, almost
got her through university
And you began it all at seventeen,
Did it despite the prejudice, the scepticism, the
horrendous start in life you gave her.

You always used to say that if she turned
eighteen and she wasn't a mother herself
Then you'd have won at teenage parenthood,
But the truth is, now she's turning twenty-three
as you're turning forty,
You're prouder of her than you ever imagined
possible.

She's been through so much.
This time twenty-three years ago,
You were heavily pregnant with her
And you didn't even know it, yet.

It feels like only yesterday she was lying limp beside you in a NICU incubator,
But now she's twirling you around the dance floor,
Your own mother-daughter fusion of highland dance and clubbing-style,
Just you.

Your tiny wee baby is all grown up, just about taller than you are,
And it happened in the blink of an eye.
She's almost six whole years older now than you were when you gave birth to her,
Can graduate this year and start her adult life responsibility-free, thank goodness.

She's been relapse-free for the last two years, as far as you're aware-
And you don't think you'll ever be able to relax completely,
But she's happier, more at peace with where she came from
Than you could ever have hoped for seven years ago.

Your work is done.
Except it isn't- not really.
You don't think you'll ever stop mothering her,

But you get to enjoy her friendship a little more,
now.

She's your best friend.
You've thought of her as your best friend since before she was even born,
Drilled it into her because you were so utterly determined she never doubted she was wanted.
But it's different, somehow, now she's grown.

You've raised her to be the best friend you never even knew you needed,
Despite the statistics, despite everything.
You love her more than you even know how to explain, and the beautiful part is,
She's twenty-two years old, but you know she still loves you right back.

When she was born, everyone told you that you just needed to get her to adulthood.
That the time goes so quickly.
That you'd have plenty of chance to reclaim your lost freedom, live your life for you,
Once she was all grown-up, independent.

And yet here you are at your fortieth birthday party,
The period of your life you dedicated to raising her coming to an end.

And yet the only way you want to spend the next chapter, and the one after it, and forever,
Is with her.

"You okay?" she asks you gently, holds your hands in hers,
Sways you with her. "Mum?"
"I'm fine. Why…"
"Are you crying?"

"Just a wee bit." You wipe at your eyes furiously.
Her face falls. "Oh no, Mum… why? Was it too much…"
"No," you reassure her. "No, nothing like that."
"Then why…"

"Why am I crying?"
"Yeah."
You pull her into your arms, hug her like it's her wedding dance,
Never want to let her go.

"Because," you tell her softly, whisper in her ear so it's just you two, together.
"Because I'm so, so proud of you."
"Awww, Mum." She pauses for a moment, contemplates. "I'm proud of you, too."
Your heart bursts.

"You really mean that?" you ask her, eyes
flooding with tears all over again
And you can't even blame the menopause,
because you only had her at seventeen.
"Of course I do," she insists. "What… how you
had me," she says quietly. "Everything you…"
"Hey, I know. I know, sweetheart. I know. It's
okay…"

"I couldn't have done what you did," she tells
you,
And you're lost in each other, oblivious to the
celidh around you,
But no part of you cares,
And you suspect no part of her does, either.

"How do you mean?"
"You know. Having me. Everything you went
through to have me." Her voice breaks.
"Hey, you're okay, darling…"
"I only got through my Highers because you
held me together…"

"No, you didn't…"
"Yes, I did," she insists. "How you did yours
with me…"
"It wasn't that bad…"

“Don’t lie. And uni. How you managed uni with me, I don’t even understand…”

“You want to know how I did it?”
She blinks at you, her father’s eyes, except they stopped belonging to him long ago. “Yeah?”
“Because I had you,” you tell her.
You run your thumb gently beneath her eyes, wipe away her tears.

“Everything I’ve managed since I turned seventeen. All of it. I did it because I had you.”

Printed by Libri Plureos GmbH in Hamburg, Germany

9 789357 444316